TRUST
SEX
HEIGHTS &
ENLIGHTENMENT

SUNDARI GRACE

TRUST
SEX
HEIGHTS &
ENLIGHTENMENT

© Sundari Grace 2019

First published in Australia in 2019 as this edition.

ISBN: 978-0-6485533-4-2 (Paperback)
ISBN: 978-0-6485533-5-9 (Hardback)

All rights reserved. Apart from any fair dealing for the purposes of private study, research, criticism or review, as permitted under copyright law, no part of this book may be reproduced by any process without written permission. Inquiries should be addressed to info@sundarigrace.com.

www.sundarigrace.com

*In loving memory of a young self
that needed who I am now.*

Step off with me

I'm waiting for you.
Standing in this box suspended on wires across a canyon,
I am ready. I am set.
But you're not here.

I'm not waiting for you.
I step off the ledge and fling myself into the arms
of air and space
and I trust myself now, like the harness that keeps me
from dying
but lets me plunge again and again to the very edges of life,
of me,
of the Goddess that is All in the freedom of falling and
safety and embracing everything I find on the way down,
and back up,
and down again.
The only risk is to the container.
I burst out of it - and on my own.

I *am* waiting for you, but not quietly.
I still want
to step off this ledge with you and plunge
to those different unknown depths that will take us to new landscapes,
new versions of ourselves, new versions, maybe, of
being human.

I step off the ledge.
Step off with me.

Pebble

I stood alone on a pebble and
my food-fuel and feeling-fuel and thinking-fuel
all ran straight to one muscle, then the next,
then the next,
balancing and
rebalancing
and rebalancing again
as life passed by and tried
to throw me this way
and that.
I believed this was living.

Then a life floated by slowly enough
and I saw a blissful, human shape
resting on it and, distracted,
I fell
and was softly caught by a life
that floats and sighs soulfully.
I rested and
my food-fuel and feeling-fuel and thinking-fuel
gathers and shoots out blazes of beauty into a
mingle with those of others.

Secret Symbol

I sought my secret symbol in the rubble
of yesterdays and myself in a trillion interactions
that happened before my consciousness enveloped them.
I was there, but I was not,
And my symbol was nowhere.

I sought my secret symbol in the chaos
of righteous writings and songs and buildings
filled with roles instead of people.
I was there, but I was not,
And my symbol was nowhere.

I sought my secret symbol in the explosions
of rolling flesh and lingams attached to fearful men
who didn't know what they possessed.
I was there, but I was not,
And my symbol was nowhere.

I sought my secret symbol in the quiet
of darkness and fullness and the
blazing light that only souls can emanate.
I was there and I was All.
And there was no symbol
nor secret.
Only I, for I am
That I Am.

Trust-Worthy Warrior

If you are trust-worthy,
a door will open
for you to fall through.

If you are gentle,
you will know the secret strength
beyond the gate.

If you are present,
embers will light into
engulfing flames.

And you will be God.

Feed the dead

A voice from the past on a telephone -
Damn the technology that remembers
everything,
thinks *everything* is worth saving.
Growth requires change,
change requires death -
the death of things that sit preserved
in servers that are overfed
but ever hungry,
and ever fed.

The scientist

It's not that I wanted to fit in
but meaning is made
and what from?

A heart you don't know yet?
A soul you're not yet sure is there?

Survival is meaning
and we eat and protect
and sleep, though we don't understand it.

Perhaps sleep and the dreams
that come drive our attempts to live
beyond survival
and the meaning that's made
before our Selves are full Sources
give us food for experiments.

I was not wrong -
I was trying it out

and recording data
and choosing relevance
and my analysis turned out
to be
no for this
yes for that
YES for these

and anything YES was what I kept.

The Queendom is Coming

Rest your soul, my love,
the Queendom is coming.

You will be safe, my love,
the Queendom is coming.

Let your joy muster, my love,
the Queendom is coming.

Adventure awaits, my love,
the Queendom is coming.

Meet me at the river

Meet me at the river
and kiss me so softly
the concrete covered bank
crumbles back into rich, dark earth
and, we, also.

Sweetheart

Come to me -
I am a safe container for you and your
sweet heart.
Honour my softness
and I will shape it around you.
Challenge my fear with love
and I will lay down my guns
and hold you.
Call on my strength
and I will carry you home.

Reunite

we live
                            together but apart
in this one world
                            pieced together like a
jigsaw
                    boundaries clear in
straight lines
                      corners and curves
marked by
          skin and cloth fences
impassable
          but we breathe the
same air
      that travels to
cells
   in separated
selves
  and reaches to
reunite

Shut the gate

I stroke my head -
in comfort,
in madness,
in pride so large
I hope it hides my fear
but fear it doesn't and
I stroke till my head is
a raw, ugly shield
I can hide behind.
I glare out of a window -
"It's open", I shout
like you're welcome -
and shut the gate.

Worlds

I yearn
and throw myself
through barriers
to find worlds
I want to exist.

Ancient trees

If I told you which moments meant most to me
your brows would curve in confusion
and the understanding words
you might have said
would stop.
Those life-giving droplets may have fallen from you unnoticed
but they dug down deep into
the earth beneath me and grew stumps
as strong as ancient trees
and the structures they hold now rise into an infinite sky.

My heart bleeds

My heart bleeds into the sky and writes names and dates and words
in which to keep you, Life, precious, loved,
strong, complete and yet growing
and spreading and filling that sky that reaches down
and kisses each new bud and old leaf and solid branch
in a passionate riot of peace and joy and heart-expanding
Love.

There is a rush and a silence, a stillness that holds me in place
and directs my light, my made things,
my Self.
Directs and yet frees into wildness,
so I can blast out like fireworks and lose my shape and
become light, in light shades and dark, but still only
Light.

Meet me in the middle

I dream of the day you've made me feel
safe enough to come
when you gently press my knees wide, and pull me
to you so that we
meet in the middle.

Please, please meet me in the middle.

Do you express how deep the pool of your desire is
or do you, cowardly, let only art tell your story
like it's not yours,
like the pool is not inside you ready to boil over,
like you can deny it if asked?
But do you not yearn to be asked?
I yearn for your answer.
And for mine.

King Cock

I am King and I follow
MY COCK
as it points its direction
choice after choice.
A woman once tapped on
the subtle compass in my chest and said 'due north' hopefully.
I scoffed 'it is a tiny needle!' and laughed
and said grandly "Why,
oh why would I want any but
MY COCK?'
and he fell into a hole
and it ate him.

Wind

I sat in my house and asked the wind to push through me.
She smiled and held a loving presence around me,
warmly still.

So I stood in the street and asked the wind to rush through me
but she whispered a loving dance around my skin,
tantalisingly gentle.

I climbed to a mountain top, hoping the wind was stronger there
but she deftly curved around me
and the mountain both.

So I leaped from a plane and the speed was my very own
and I pushed through the wind and she pushed through me,
Cleansing

and sweetly whispering 'I needed your choice to be clear'.

The health I have

Vitality jumps
up and down
in cells made mostly of
space -
anything but imprisoned -
driving a giant
human-shaped
conglomeration
of teamwork
through a life of
daily creation.

Speed

A thousand miles an hour
and I drink stillness into my heart
like liquid pause.
Speed.
My body drives through space - a vehicle inside a vehicle -
and I inside them both,
a silent passenger with no control
and no wish to.
Cells relax away from each other and my body becomes
lighter
larger
sweeter.
The experience paints a new picture of me and
I sit in myself a little better now.

The car screeches left and my delicious, liquid stillness is
thrown out to the right;
it reaches a limit and springs back
to my heart centre:
I learn that I am anchored by an elastic leash and
that ecstasy can roll out in waves from places
you can't touch with hands or finger tips or the lingams
human men carry with them everywhere they go.
Why is it that cars, and not men, have learnt to
reach here?

Monster - Goddess

A monster reaches, open-mouthed
and vast as a shadow over beauty,
over me.
I do not know you.
But the unknown sits in my ignorance,
not your nature,
and my blind eyes grow open -
protective mother reaches, open-armed
and vast as a goddess's heart over beauty,
over me,
until I'm ready.

The Pink Flag

I followed the pink flag -
the colour of flowers and ribbons
and other instruments of love.
But somewhere on the road,
bloody and bruised,
I caught up to it
and with swollen eyes
and a scarred brain
I stared at the flag -
red on one side,
the other white.

Wild Delight

The dogs are howling - their song
travels through a neighbourhood made
sleepy by the first heat of summer,
pierces the walls of my quiet house and
shoots into my chest like a lightning flash
from Mother Witch's wand.
My heart explodes like a science experiment
gone wrong
and I am found, a wolf leading my
dog from its tameness
and relishing in my newfound
wild delight.

Thy Queendom Come

Our Divine God/dess, who art Everywhere,
Hallowed be Thy Many Names.
Thy Queendom come,
Thy will be done in the
Causal, Astral and Physical realms.
Give us this day our daily dose of experiences.
Always give us the Grace to come back from
Our wrong choices
And help us to cultivate this same Grace
Towards others.
Lead us into temptation after temptation
With deep, penetrative consciousness
And deepen our consciousness with your own.
For the Queendom, the Power, and the Glory are
Yours, Ours, All,
In all past, present and future that is always
The Eternal Now.

Risk

We face possible death going to the
supermarket, and harm
when we meet a new face.
If you see the risk I'm taking,
and I see yours,
where will our hearts be?

The alley

You held me up against a
brick wall
and loved me four times:
once for safety
once for sweetness
once for depth
and once for a heaven
of Oneness we
found in an alley,
running from a spire
we didn't need.

Aim

I stand at your front door and press the button -
my car clicks open.

I wait.

I press again - *click* -
and wait.

I look down at the button in my hand through
the blur of tears

and click again.

Soft

I want to touch your skin
with a soft heart
to see if it is as hard
as you try to make it.

I said to the Lady in the Walls...

Am I mad, then, that I see you?
Is that the only measure of madness
in this room with four walls and a
vent I wouldn't fit through?
But you did, didn't you?
Or were you born here,
in these walls,
and know how to travel them freely?

And are you stuck or are you
living life as you desire it -
climbing through vents and
pressing face-shaped artworks into
plaster walls that tell the stories
of your days?
If I climbed through the vent,
and made it,
only to rescue you,
would you thank me or rile at me
in baffled anger, that I would take you away
from this, your beloved existence?

And am I mad that I question my sanity
based only on the seen?
Does sight,
and not love or hatred,
or the choice of
violence over sweetness,
determine the loss of a mind,
of a being?

A being - and are you human, then?
If I, also human,
climbed through the vent,
and made it,
only to join you, perhaps even
Love you,
would you thank me or rile at me
in baffled despair that I would not rescue you
from this, your imprisoned existence?
But how can I, mad as I am, rescue you?

Rabbit hole

Lover, I see you
throwing yourself head-first from planes,
slamming your foot on accelerators,
diving deeper than a breath will take you
into an ocean of sharks.
Why do you avoid this rabbit hole?
There's a heart in it somewhere.

I Am Persephone

I fall, not just willingly -
I searched with bare, broken feet
for the entrance to this
dark world where the lies and truths
kept hidden
will be my freedom, my power.

Men painted me pretty to save
their fragile, selfish eyes
but I needed it not -
I needed the beauty of digging
with bleeding hands
and a determination that opened
the earth to swallow me whole
and make me Herself.

The pomegranate was Mine;
Hades simply did as I asked
and passed it to me.

Spider, spider

Spider, Spider on the wall,
Spider, teach me how to crawl.
I tried to run, I tried to walk,
Oh Spider, all I did was fall.

Spider, closer, come to me.
Spider, help my eyes to see.
Though only two, I do believe,
Oh Spider, like yours, mine can be.